Slimer's G

CW00726259

In THE REAL GHOSTBUSTERS series

SLIMER'S GHOULISH GAGS

JONATHAN CLEMENTS

CARNIVAL

Carnival
An imprint of the Children's Division
of the Collins Publishing Group,
8 Grafton Street, London W1X 3LA

Published by Carnival 1988
Reprinted 1989

ISBN 0 00 194300 6

Printed and bound in Great Britain by
Collins, Glasgow

Set in Times

SLIMER'S GHOULISH GAGS

~THE FIRST REVOLTING DOLLOP~

JANINE: Hey, Slimer, what's that dreadful, hideous, unspeakable monstrosity on your shoulders

SLIMER: Glub! What! Help! Help . . .!

JANINE: Oh relax, dumbo. It's just your head.

PETER: Guess who writes a ghoul-comedian's jokes for him.

RAY: Give up. Who does?

PETER: Easy – a crypt writer!

EGON: I think I'd like to get some new equipment for the lab. I need an electric neutron scanner, an electrically-powered shredder, an electric micro-drill for classifying particles . . .

RAY: You're crazy about electricity, aren't you, Egon?

EGON: I suppose I am, yes.

RAY: Do you know what that makes you?

EGON: What?

RAY: Oh, an electric fan!

JANICE: I'm reading this lovely romantic story about a girl vampire who falls in love with a boy vampire.

PETER: Love at first bite, eh?

EGON: What's a ghoul's favourite soup?

RAY: Scream of chicken.

WINSTON: What do you call a ghoul who buzzes people's doorbells?

RAY: A dead ringer.

The Real Ghostbusters had cornered a wicked ghost in a pyjama factory, and with his proton gun ready for action, Peter sprang up the staircase towards where the ghoul was hiding. Before he reached the top, the ghost, with a hideous laugh, appeared in a swirl of mist and cried:

'Okay, guys, I know when I'm licked. I'll surrender.'

'Good show,' said Egon.

'There's just one thing,' added the ghost, 'do you think I could have one request before you dispose of me.'

'What is it?' said Peter.

'It's not much to ask; I'd just like to sing a song.'

'Okay,' said Peter, 'Go ahead.'

'There were seven hundred million green bottles,' sang the ghost, 'hanging on the wall . . .'

JANINE: Egon took me dancing last night, and he said I looked like an Italian dish.

PETER: Well, you *do*, Janine!

JANINE: Why, thank you, Peter. Who did you have in mind – Sophia Loren?

PETER: No – spaghetti bolognaise!

Peter arrived at a seaside hotel in Brighton very late at night. He was on the trail of a ghost named Glop, and had made the reservation at the last moment. All the hotel lights were out when Peter strode up and knocked on the door.

After a long wait, a light appeared in an upstairs window, a woman poked her head out and called:

'Who are you? What do you want at this unearthly hour?'

'I'm Peter Venkman, Ghostbuster. I'm staying here for the night.'

'Okay,' said the woman, slamming the window closed. 'You stay there, then!'

JANINE: Hey, Slimer! Do you know what I'd do if I had a face like yours?

SLIMER: Glug – grunt – what?

JANINE: I'd sue for damages . . . No, but seriously, Slimer, there's only one thing wrong with your face.

SLIMER: Glug – splaat – what's that?

JANINE: It shows.

PETER: Did you hear about the werewolf ghost who did a turn on a TV comedy show?

EGON: No. How did he make out?

PETER: Really well. He had the audience screaming and howling with laughter.

After a particularly harrowing adventure, during which The Real Ghostbusters had rounded up a malicious spirit which had terrified the entire population of a monastery in Moscow, the gang flopped to have a well-earned rest in the lounge at Headquarters.

'Tell me, Peter,' said Egon Spengler. 'Every day we seem to flirt with danger and death – are you ever scared?'

Peter Venkman shrugged his shoulders. 'Well, I suppose every now and then I am.'

Up piped the irrepressible Ray Stantz, 'Hey, I'm not a bit scared of death.'

'You're not?' said the others.

'Nope,' winked Ray. 'I'm not at all scared of dying – I just don't want to be there when it happens!'

RAY: I hear Janine is becoming quite a lady private eye.

PETER: Yeah . . . she's sort of a slick chick dick.

TV INTERVIEWER:	Are there any particular ghosts you've caught that stick in your memory?
EGON:	Well, there was this horrible ghost of a vampire in Transylvania . . .
PETER:	Yeah, he was truly monstrous. Do you know what he'd say to his victims after he'd sucked all the blood from their throats?
TV INTERVIEWER:	No, what?
PETER:	Well, fangs very much!

RAY: I think Janine uses too much make-up.

WINSTON: What makes you say that, Ray?

RAY: Well, it's so thick that for ten minutes after she's stopped laughing at something, her face is still set in a smile.

PETER: Hey, Slimer, what do you do when your nose goes on strike?

SLIMER: Glub . . . blug . . . Errr . . . picket.

WINSTON: What has twelve legs, six ears and one eye?

EGON: Ugh! Sounds like a pretty ghastly ghoul.

WINSTON: Nope. Three blind mice and half a kipper!

EGON: You're rather odiferous, Slimer.
           Have you washed lately?
SLIMER: Blub . . . course I have.
EGON: Well, I have my doubts. In fact, I
           think you're not doing all you
           could in the way of personal
           hygiene.
SLIMER: Mblog . . . look, Egon, I'll have
           you know I take a bath every six
           months – whether I need it or not!

PETER:	I didn't always want to be a Ghostbuster, you know.
WINSTON:	Really? What else did you want to do?
PETER:	I had a driving ambition to be an actor.
WINSTON:	And did you appear in anything, Peter?
PETER:	Just a few small parts. Still, I'll always remember my first lines in a theatre.
WINSTON:	What were they?
PETER:	'Peanuts, ice-lollies . . .'

RAY: You know those alterations on the proton guns I thought needed doing? Well, I've changed my mind.

JANINE: Oh, good. Does it work any better than the old one?

JANINE: Say, Peter – did you manage to capture that dreadful ghost who was going around eating people?

PETER: Yep.

JANINE: Great. And what did the horrible fiend say when The Ghostbusters arrived on the scene in their new souped-up turbo train?

PETER: Oh, that ghost was pretty confident he was going to chew us all up and spit out the bones. All it said was 'Mmmmm, goody . . . a chew-chew train!'

WINSTON: What are you reading there, Ray?

RAY: It's a copy of Count Dracula's school report, and it's fascinating stuff.

WINSTON: I bet. How did he do at school anyway?

RAY: Well, it says here . . . 'Reading; good . . . Writing; untidy . . . Cricket; shows definite promise as a bat . . .'

PETER: Now give me a frank answer, Janine – what do you really think of me?

JANINE: Well, Peter, I think you have a big heart . . .

PETER: Gosh, that's really nice of you . . .

JANINE: Wait, I hadn't finished. I was about to say you had a big heart . . . and a head to match.

| WINSTON: | Peter, what's Count Dracula's address when he's staying in New York? |
| PETER: | Why, the Vampire State Building! |

RAY:	Is it true, Winston, that you're really into fortune-telling?
WINSTON:	I sure am.
RAY:	And you dig mediums and clairvoyants and seances?
WINSTON:	That's right.
RAY:	And you place a great deal of faith in your star sign and stuff like that?
WINSTON:	Yeah, it so happens I do.
RAY:	And every day without fail you check your horoscope in the paper to see where it's all at?
WINSTON:	So what? Look, Ray, what exactly are you driving at?
RAY:	Well, Winston, it's just as I figured – you're nothing but a seer-sucker.

EGON: Who's at the door, Janine?
JANINE: It's the Invisible Man for you.
EGON: Gosh, I'm so mixed up in this exper-
          iment . . . Tell him I'm too busy;
          tell him I can't see him today.

Hot on the trail of a ghoul who dabbled in cannibalism, Peter was flying over the Peruvian jungle when the plane suddenly developed engine trouble. He got into his parachute, jumped, pulled the rip-chord and drifted slowly down to the ground.

As luck would have it, Peter crashed through the trees and landed smack in the middle of a large boiling cauldron which was being stirred by the cannibal ghoul.

'Waiter, my compliments to the chef,' said the ghoul, with a fiendish chuckle. 'There's a flyer in my soup.'

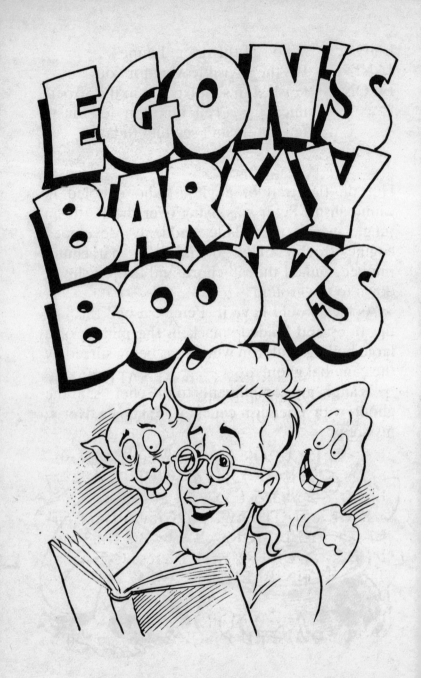

EGON'S BARMY BOOKS

'THE HAUNTED HOUSE' by Hugo First
'CONFESSIONS OF A MUGGER' by Ann Dover
'EXPLOSIVES & PRACTICAL SAFE-BLOWING' by Dinah Mite.
'A HISTORY OF OLD FURNITURE' by Anne Teak
'BANBURY CROSS' by Rhoda Whitehorse
'SMACKED BOTTOMS' by Ben Dover
'FEEDING MONKEYS' by P. Nuts
'HIGHER MATHEMATICS' by Adam Upp
'BRICKS AND MORTAR' by Bill Ding
'IN THE COUNTRY' by Theresa Greene
'THE WIND BLEW IT AWAY' by Lydia Dustbin
'HOW TO WARM ROOMS' by Ray D. Ater
'WHY YOU NEED INSURANCE' by Justin Case

'THE GREAT ESCAPE' by Freda Convict
'HOW I MADE A MILLION POUNDS' by Jack Pott
'THE FLOWER GARDEN' by Polly Anthus
'IT'S QUITE IMPOSSIBLE' by Freyda Cant
'CHRISTMAS PLANTS' by Miss L. Toe.
'THE WEDGED DOOR' by Paul Hard
'HORNED ANIMALS' by Ann T. Lope
'THE ILL-FITTING SHOE' by Ivor Blister
'PRACTICAL RICE GROWING' by Paddy Fields

'SPICY MEATS AND FUNNY SAUS-AGES' by Della Katessen

'GROWING YOUR OWN VEGETA-BLES' by Rosa Carrots

'ACHES AND PAINS' by Arthur Itis

'THE P. S.' by Adeline Moore

'GETTING RICH IN A HURRY' by Robin Banks

'ESCAPE OF THE KILLER BULL' by Gay Topen

'THE STORY OF INSOMNIA' by Eliza Wake

'THE ENGLISH LANGUAGE' by Dick Shunnry

'OFF TO MARKET' by Tobias A. Pigg

'PUNCTURED' by Buster Tyre

'A QUESTION OF DOUBT' by Willie Wontie

'JAPANESE WEEKEND' by Sat Sun Mon

'WEARY LEGS' by Carrie Mee-Home

'IS THIS THE WAY OUT?' by Isadora Nexit

'AROUND THE MOUNTAIN' by Sheila B. Cummin

'POUR ME A DRINK' by Bart Ender

'STAMP OUT CRIME & EVIL' by Laura Norder

'TIME TO GO TO SCHOOL' by R. U. Upyett

'PLAYING IN AN ORCHESTRA' by Vy O'Lynn

'A BRICK FELL ON MY HEAD' by I. C. Stars

'DISEASES OF THE HAIR' by Dan Druff

'CERTAINTIES' by R. U. Shaw

'BABYSITTING FOR FUN & PROFIT' by Justin Casey Howells

'SUMMER HOLIDAY' by C. Side

'FIVE BABIES' by Bertha Quinns

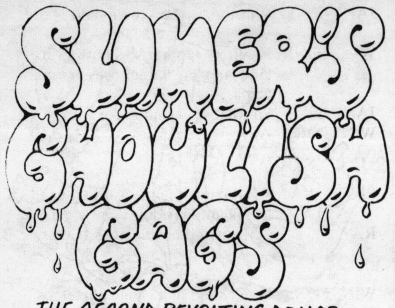

SLIMER'S GHOULISH GAGS

—THE SECOND REVOLTING DOLLOP—

JANINE: Winston, what nationality are you?

WINSTON: Well, my mother was born in Iceland and my father was born in Cuba.

JANINE: So what does that make you?

WINSTON: An ice-cube, I guess.

PETER: What kind of horse was that headless phantom riding?

RAY: Oh, a nightmare.

WINSTON: Don't sit in that chair, Slimer.

SLIMER: Glug . . . Why not?

WINSTON: It's for rigor mortis to set in.

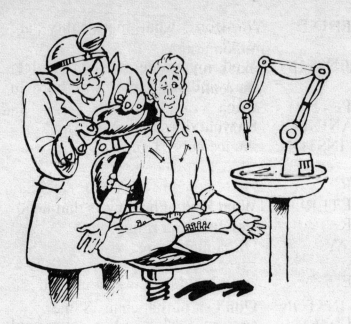

PETER: I went to the dentist yesterday.
WINSTON: Yeah? That's tough.
PETER: Sure was. He wanted to pull out two teeth.
WINSTON: Did it hurt?
PETER: No. I wouldn't let him do it.
WINSTON: Why not?
PETER: Well, I wanted to transcend dental medication.

WINSTON: I've been thinking of crossing a telescope with a vampire.
JANINE: Whatever for?
WINSTON: I might come up with a good horrorscope!

PETER: You know, Janine, you look like a million dollars.

JANINE: That's really nice of you, Pete. Do you really mean it?

PETER: Sure. You look all green and crinkly . . .

RAY: Where do monsters go for a holiday?

EGON: I don't know. Where?

RAY: Lake Erie!

EGON: Well, Janine, how's your new diet going?

JANINE: The one where I'm only only allowed to eat onions? Not too good; I've lost a stone . . . and all my friends!

RAY: Is that new guy Phelps stupid?

PETER: I'll say he is! He's so stupid he couldn't tell which way a lift was going, even if he had two guesses!

RAY: . . . and then we started to battle against Glop, the monster who was taking all the chat show hosts and rendering them dumb.

JANINE: I would have thought that was a blessing.

RAY: It was, but unfortunately against the law. Anyway, I zapped Glop with my proton gun and fired a stream of high energy ions into him.

JANINE: Then what happened?

RAY: It was really weird; his left hand fell off and disintegrated.

JANINE: Oh, no! What did he do?

RAY: He was all right. On the way back to the ecto-containment unit, he stopped off at a second-hand store.

Peter's Delirious Dictionary

A

ABANDON: What a hat sometimes has.

ACCORD: A thick piece of string.

ACE: Frozen water found in Kensington.

ACROBAT: A person who breaks his back to fill his belly.

ADDRESS: Something that girls wear but boys don't.

ACQUIRE: A group of singers.

AIRSPACE: A bald patch.

ALLOCATE: What you say when you meet somebody called Kate.

ALONE: In bad company.

AMBIDEXTROUS: Able to pick a pocket with either hand.

B

BATTALION: One of the divisions in the vampires' army.

BIRDHOUSE: Home tweet home.

BISON: What a father says when he leaves his boy.

BORE: A person who talks when you want them to listen.

C

CALVES: Animals that follow you every step.

CANNIBAL: Someone who is fed up with people.

CLOAK: The sound a Chinese frog makes.

D

DEBATE: Used for luring fish to a hook.

DENIAL: An Egyptian river.

DEPRESSANT : A miserable insect.

DIVINE: Where de grapes grow.

DOCTOR: A person who thrives on diseases, and could well die of good-health.

DRY-DOCK: A very thirsty surgeon.

E

EAVESDROP: Adam's wife listening to gossip.

ECLIPSE: What a gardener does to a hedge.

EUROPE: Piece of string belonging to you.

EXTINCT: A dead skunk.

F

FANFARE:	An exhibition of fans.
FELON:	Dropped from above.
FIB:	A lie that has not grown up.
FLEA:	An insect that has gone to the dogs.
FLAW:	Opposite to the ceiling.
FOUL LANGUAGE:	Swearing in the chicken-coop.

G

GALLOWS:	A place where no noose is good noose.
GAS-METER:	The family liar under the stairs.
GRAVELY:	How most spooks speak.
GOOSE:	A bird that grows down as it grows up.
GUILLOTINE:	A device which makes a Frenchman shrug his shoulders with very good reason.

H

HATCHET:	What a hen does with an egg.
HOT-DOG:	A pet who sat too close to the fire.
HEDGEHOG:	A cactus on four legs.
HISTORIAN:	A long-range gossip.
HOMESICK:	To be flat-broke when abroad.

I
ICE-CREAM: To yell at the top of my voice.
IMPECCABLE: Something chickens can't eat.
INKLING: A baby fountain pen.
INTENSE: Where boy scouts sleep.

J

JARGON: A container is missing.

JUMP: The last word in aeroplanes.

JUICY: Did you notice that?

JURY: Twelve ignorant people who suddenly achieve wisdom.

K

KIDNAP: What a baby has after lunch and dinner.

KIDNEY: What a young goat kneels on.

KNOB: Something to adore.

L

LAUNCH: A mid-day meal for astronauts.

LAUGHING-STOCK: Gravy that has a sense of humour.

LISP: When you call a spade a thspade

LAPLANDER: Somebody who keeps falling over in trains and buses.

36

M

MARIGOLD: A woman who weds for money.

MARKET: What a teacher does with homework.

MEANTIME: A particularly nasty clock.

MOTEL: William Tell's sister.

MYTH: An unmarried moth.

N

NEUROSIS: Very fresh flowers.

NIGHTINGALE: A wild and stormy evening.

NORMALISE: Pretty good vision.

NOTICABLE: To spot a male cow.

NOISE: A stink in the ear.

O

OHM: No place like it, they say.

OLIVE: Where you usually reside.

OYSTER: What you shout when somebody starts to lift your teacher high in the air with a crane.

P

PARADOX:	Two surgeons.
PANTHER:	Somebody who makes panths.
PICKET:	What to do to your nose.
PEDESTRIAN:	The audible part of a road that a car travels over.
POSITIVE:	To be mistaken at the top of one's voice.

Q

QUACK:	A duck's doctor
QUARTZ:	Four to the gallon.
QUOTA:	Repeating what a woman has said.

R

RAGTIME:	Music you dance to when your clothes wear out.
RASH PREDICTION:	A forecast, such as: 'You will have measles.'
RESIDENT:	Unable to leave.
REVOLVING DOOR:	A place to go around with people.
ROCKET:	The best way to get a baby to go to sleep.

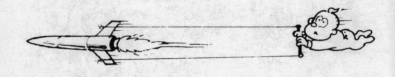

S

SAFETY:	A drink that won't harm you.
SAGO:	How you start a pudding-eating race.
SOURPUSS:	A cat who has just eaten a lemon.
SELF:	The most important person in the universe.

T

'TAINT:	It is not.
TEMPER:	Something you can lose and still have.
TORTOISE:	What our teacher did.
TULIPS:	What you kiss with.
TURTLE:	A lizard with a mobile home on its back.

U

UNAWARE:	Clothes that you put on first.
UNIT:	A term of abuse; insult.
URCHIN:	The lower part of a woman's face.
URGENT:	The same woman's boyfriend

V

VERTIGO: The question you ask someone before setting out on a journey.

VESTRY: A large plant on which you grow vests.

VICIOUS CIRCLE: A very bad-tempered geometrical figure.

VISCOUNT: Asking Violet to add up.

W

WATER: Thirst aid.

WAGGING TAIL: A happy ending.

WHOSE: Where a Scotsman lives.

X

X: What hens lay from time to time.

X-RAY: Belly-Vision.

Y

YANK: How American dentists pull teeth.

YOKEL: Somebody who laughs at yolks.

Z

ZEBRA: A horse wearing venetian blinds.

ZINC: Where you wash up.

ZING: What you do with a zong.

Janine's Loopy Limericks

When Peter took a trip to Sarum,
His manners were quite harum-scarum;
He went shopping for eggs
With no pants on his legs,
Till the fuzz compelled him to wear 'em.

From Number 8, Balaclava Mews,
There is really abominable news;
They've discovered a head
In the box for the bread . . .
And nobody seems to know whose.

An old ghost's crotchets and quibblings
Were a terrible trial to his siblings;
But he was not removed
Till one day it was proved
That the dustbin was damp with his dribblings.

While travelling in far-off Tibet,
Egon had much cause to regret
The stale cakes for tea,
A pain in his knee,
And the horrible tourists he met.

At the Villa Demented, the sleepers,
Are disturbed by a phantom in weepers;
It beats all night long
A dirge on a gong,
As it staggers about in the creepers.

Peter, in a household quite charmless,
Was informed that its owner was harmless:
'If you're caught unawares,
At the head of the stairs,
Just remember – he's eyeless and armless.'

Every night Grandpa fills me with dread,
When he sits at the foot of the bed;
I don't care that he squeaks
In gibbers and squeaks –
But for twenty two years he's been dead . . .

There was a young chap, name of Fred,
Who spent every weekday in bed;
He lay with his feet
Outside of the sheet,
And the pillows on top of his head.

As the Ghostbusters inspected the apse,
An ominous series of raps
Came from under the altar,
Which caused some to falter,
And others to shriek and collapse.

'My trip? it was vile; San Parava
I loathed; Etna was crawling with lava;
The ship was all right,
But it shuddered one night,
And it sank off the coast of East Java.'

There was a young lady named Rose,
Who fainted whenever she chose;
She did so one day,
While playing croquet,
But was quickly revived with a hose.

Janine, who weighed many an ounce,
Used language one dare not pronounce,
When Ray, quite unkind,
Pulled her chair out behind,
Just to see, so he said, if she'd bounce.

There was an old spinster from Fife,
Who had never been kissed in her life;
When along came a pig,
And she cried, 'Let's kiss and jog!'
But the pig answered, 'Not on your life!'

Egon grew increasingly peaky,
In a house where the hinges were squeaky:
The ferns curled up brown,
The ceilings fell down,
And all of the taps, they were leaky.

Once Peter was seized with intent,
to revise his existence mis-spent.
So he climbed up the dome
Of St Peter's in Rome,
Where he stayed through following Lent.

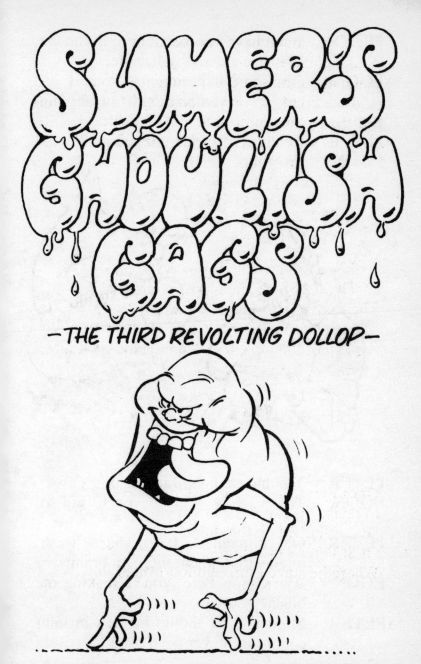

SLIMER'S GHOULISH GAGS

—THE THIRD REVOLTING DOLLOP—

PETER: What have you been up to in the lab, Egon?

EGON: Oh, some experiments, Pete. I just crossed a vampire with an abominable snowman.

PETER: Really? And what did you get?

EGON: Frostbite!

PETER: You have a fine brain, Egon.

EGON: That's really swell of you to say so, Pete.

PETER: Oh, I mean it. It's a sharp, fresh, intellectual, keen, incisive, brain.

EGON: Aw, c'mon Pete, you're making me blush.

PETER: Mind you, it should be. It's in mint condition; never been used.

RAY: Why are members of a vampire family so very close to each other?

PETER: Because blood is thicker than water.

EGON: Oh, gosh, I just did an awful experiment, and I feel sick at the stomach.

WINSTON: What have you been up to now, Dr Frankenstein?

EGON: Well, I thought I'd cross a midget with a vampire.

WINSTON: Uh-huh. And dare we ask what you came up with?

EGON: Oh, it was horrible . . . I got a little fiend who sucked all the blood out of my kneecaps!

PETER: Look out! There's a Ghostway on your back!

EGON: What's a Ghostway?

PETER: Not a lot, not a lot.

PETER: You know, Winston, ghosts are really pretty simple things.

WINSTON: How did you work that out, Pete?

PETER: Well, you can see right through them!

RAY: Hey, Winston, is it true you've been to see a new fortune-teller?

WINSTON: That's right, man. And she was really wild! She was dancing all over the table when she read the cards, laughing all the time, cracking jokes, singing jolly songs, stuff like that.

RAY: She sounds like a nutcase. What kind of a clairvoyant behaves like that?

WINSTON: Well, I guess she was a happy medium.

JANINE: Say, Egon . . . you'd better keep your eyes open tomorrow.

EGON: Why's that?

JANINE: Well, if you don't, you'll bump into everything.

1ST GHOUL
MOTHER: Mercy me, hasn't your little girl grown!

2ND GHOUL
MOTHER: Yep, she's certainly gruesome.

PETER: Why do ghosts paint their knee-caps flourescent blue?

EGON: I don't know . . . why?

PETER: So they can hide in blue jeans.

EGON: That's rubbish, and I don't believe it.

PETER: But have you ever seen a ghost in blue jeans?

EGON: Well, no . . .

PETER: You see, it works!

RAY: I had terrible eyesight until I was sixteen . . . I couldn't see a thing.

WINSTON: That's awful. What happened when you were sixteen . . . did you have an operation?

RAY: No. I had my fringe cut.

1ST GHOUL:	Hey, did you see that? That pretty girl monster over there just rolled her eyes at me.
2ND GHOUL:	You'd better roll them right back – she might be needing them again.

JANINE:	I've been popular ever since I was a little girl.
RAY:	I bet.
JANINE:	I have too. I just wish I had a penny for every time I've been asked out.
RAY:	Well, at least you'd be able to go to the toilet, if nothing else.

PETER:	Where does the Bride of Frank- enstein have her hair done?
RAY:	At the Ugly Parlour.

RAY: I saw Frankenstein in a storm last night. A terrific bolt of lightning crashed down and reverberated right through his heart.

WINSTON: Wow! What did Frankenstein say?

RAY: He said: 'Thanks; I sure needed that!'

EGON: Hey, Janine, what happened to that undertaker you were going steady with for a time?

JANINE: Oh, he retired and buried himself in the country.

JANINE: I just don't know what to make of Slimer.

PETER: How about a casserole?

DOCTOR: I'm terribly sorry, Slimer, but tests we have made prove that you have rabies.

SLIMER: Glob . . . Gimme pen and paper.

DOCTOR: Why, do you wish to make a will?

SLIMER: No . . . glub-glub . . . I wanna make a list of the people I wanna bite.

Peter and Winston were crawling through a cave in Transylvania, hot on the trail of a gang of murdering zombies. Suddenly there was a terrifying series of screams, and a weird luminous shape floated out of the murk and attacked Peter. He gave a wail of agony and yelled:

'Arrrrggggh! That ghost just bit off my leg!'

'Oh, no,' said Winston. 'Which one?'

'I don't know,' moaned Peter. 'You see one ghost and you've seen them all!'

PETER: I saw something floating in the North Sea, shouting: 'Knickers! Rhubarb! Bottoms! Bogies! Knickers!'

JANINE: How awful. What was it?

PETER: Crude oil.

DOCTOR: Did those tablets I gave you help you sleep any better?

RAY: Not really. You made a mistake – instead of sleeping tablets, you gave me arsenic!

DOCTOR: Dear me, I'm dreadfully sorry, Ray. That'll be another £2.50.

EGON: I was sorry to hear about the death of your husband, Elspeth.

ELSPETH: Yes, it was a tragic blow.

EGON: How did he actually die?

ELSPETH: Well, it was very quick. He went into the garden to cut a cabbage for dinner, bent down, and suddenly died.

EGON: That's awful. Whatever did you do?

ELSPETH: What else could I do? I had to open a can of beans.

PETER: My grandfather's given me his goat to look after.

JANINE: Well, you can't keep it here at Headquarters. What about the dreadful smell?

PETER: That's all right, Janine. The goat won't mind.

Ray was on holiday in Brighton, leaning over the rail of the pier, when a woman stumbled and fell over the rails. She landed with a splash in the deep sea, and shouted to Ray above:

'Please, drop me a line!'

'Sure,' said Ray. 'What's your address?'

PETER: Hey, Ghost – how did you break your leg?

GHOST: I trod on a cigarette to put it out.

PETER: How on earth did you break your leg just doing that?

GHOST: I dropped it in an open manhole, then stepped on it.

EGON: That carpet I bought is in mint condition.

RAY: Yeah, sure . . . it's got a hole in the middle.

JANINE: I have the complexion of a teenager.

RAY: You'd better give it back – you're getting it all wrinkled.

GIRL
SKELETON: Do you love me?

BOY
SKELETON: Every bone in your body, babe.

WINSTON: Excuse me, ma'am, but your husband just fell into the well in your back garden.

WOMAN: Oh, that doesn't matter, nobody drinks the water from there anymore . . .

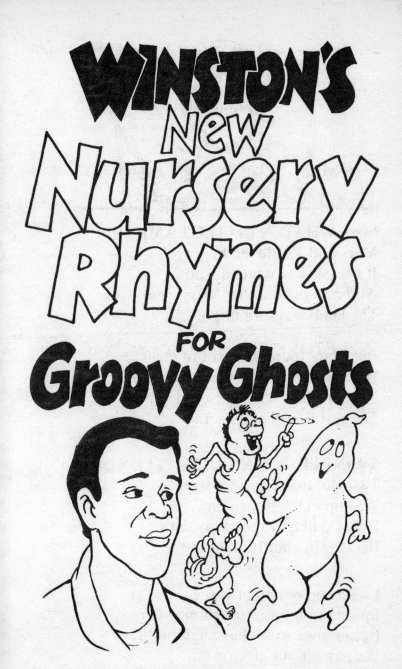

WINSTON'S New Nursery Rhymes FOR Groovy Ghosts

MARY HAD A LITTLE LAMB
Mary had a little lamb,
It's fleece was white as snow;
And everywhere that Mary went,
The lamb was sure to go.

But Mary found the cost of meat
Had soared, which didn't please her;
Tonight she's having leg of lamb –
The rest is in the freezer.

TWINKLE, TWINKLE, LITTLE STAR
Twinkle, twinkle, little star,
Way up in the sky so far;
How I'd like to spend my days,
Basking in your brilliant rays.

I wish and pray that you were near,
Inside our house, just shining here;
Because we won't have light until
We pay off our electric bill.

CHRISTOPHER ROBIN

Hush, hush,
Nobody cares,
Christopher Robin
Has fallen downstairs.

TWEEDLEDUM & TWEEDLEDEE

Tweedledum and Tweedledee,
The government called in;
To solve the economic mess,
And told them to begin.

They talked of things like price controls,
As only experts can,
Until, one day, they both agreed,
They had the perfect plan.

'There's just one way,' they told the Press,
'It's always worked before;
To solve the economic mess
We need a nice long war!'

THERE WAS AN OLD WOMAN

There was an old woman,
Who lived in a shoe,
She said, 'With my pension,
It's all I can do.

'It may be sub-standard,
But just down the block,
I know an old woman,
Who lives in a sock!'

LITTLE JACK HORNER

Little Jack Horner
Sat in a corner,
Eating a banana-split;
He put in a fist,
And pulled out a list,
Of all the E Numbers in it.

JENNY, SWEET JENNY
Jenny, sweet Jenny,
Kept every old penny,
She hoards them and nobody can stop her;
She's showing good sense
'Cause she's found that old pence
Are worth twice their value in copper.

SIMPLE SIMON
Simple Simon
Met a pie-man,
And asked him,
'What's the price?'
'Fifty pence,' replied
The pie-man,
'For a single slice.'
'Inflationary!'
Simon screamed;
'My business you
Are losing.'
The pie-man shrugged;
'I'd charge much more,
If real meat I was using.'

JACK AND JILL

Jack and Jill
Went up the hill,
On their weekly shopping
Expedition;

Jack came down,
Wearing a frown –
He'd had to swop Jill
For provisions.

HIGGLEDY PIGGLEDY

Higgledy piggledy,
My black hen,
She lays eggs
For gentlemen.
You cannot persuade her,
With gun or lariat,
To lay them
For the proletariat.

More of Janine's Loopy Limericks

There was an old lady from China,
Who once went to sea on a liner
She fell off the deck,
And twisted her neck,
And now she can see right behind her.

A timid young lady name Jane
Found parties a terrible strain,
With movements uncertain,
She'd hide in a curtain,
And make sounds like a rhino in pain.

The Dowager Duchess of Sprout,
Collapsed at the height of a rout;
As they bore her away,
She found strength to say:
'I should never have eaten the trout.'

A strange old lady named Gravell
Had often occasion to travel;
On the way she would sit,
And furiously knit;
And on the way back she'd unravel.

The sight of his guests filled Lord Bray
At breakfast with horrid dismay;
So he launched off the spoons,
The stones from his prunes,
At their heads, as they neared the buffet.

An aggressive young lady named Flunnery,
Rejoiced in the practise of gunnery;
Till one day, unobservant,
She blew up a servant,
And was forced to retire to a nunnery.

At whist-drives and strawberry teas,
Bess would giggle and show off her knees;
But when she was alone,
She'd draw on a scone,
And swing from the branches of trees.

A Victorian father named Spudgeon,
Whose kids provoked him to high dudgeon,
Used on Saturday nights,
To turn off the lights,
And chase them around with a bludgeon.

There was an old gossip named Baird,
Who said, 'What I could say, if I dared!
'I will say it in fact,
Though I die in the act . . .'
So he said it, and nobody cared.

Cried Janine who, upon a divan,
Was kissed by a naughty young man:
'Such excess of passion
Is quite out of fashion!'
And she fractured his arm with her fan.

A certain young ghoul, it was noted,
Went about in the heat thickly-coated.
He moaned, 'You may scoff,
But I shan't take it off . . .
Underneath, parts are horribly bloated.'

There was a young lady named Beager,
Who was terribly, terribly eager
To be all the rage,
On the theatrical stage,
But her talents were pitifully meagre.

Emily Prune, motivated by spite,
Tied her baby brother to a kite;
She launched it with ease,
On the afternoon breeze,
And watched till it flew out of sight.

A peculiar sportsman named Peel,
Took a trip through the sewers on his wheel;
He pedalled for days,
Through a yellowish haze,
And returned feeling somewhat unreal.

A dreary young bank clerk named Dennis
Wished to assume an aura of menace;
To make people afraid,
He wore a mask of black suede,
And white footwear intended for tennis.

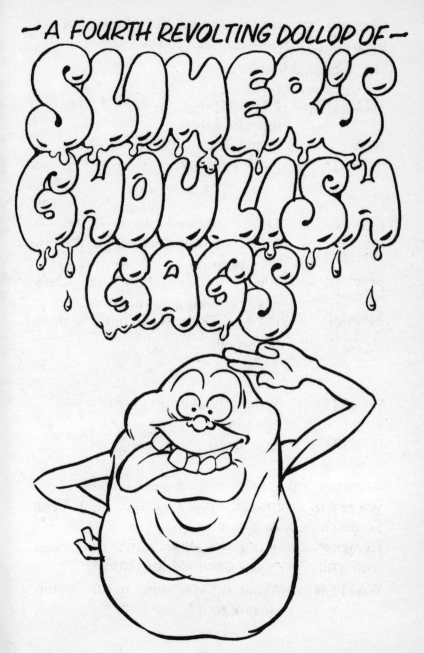

—A FOURTH REVOLTING DOLLOP OF—

SLIMER'S GHOULISH GAGS

Slimer is so unpopular that the phone doesn't even ring for him when he's in the bath.

WINSTON: I feel strange. I think I can see into the future.
RAY: When did this start?
WINSTON: Next Tuesday.

EGON: Have you seen Slimer doing his farmyard impressions – they're very unusual.
PETER: What's unusual about that – he's always making animal noises?
EGON: He doesn't do the sounds, he does the smells . . .

WINSTON: What mistakes do ghosts make?
RAY: Give in.
WINSTON: Boo-Boos.

WAITER: Here's the leg of lamb you ordered, Madam.
JANINE: Is it English lamb, or New Zealand?
WAITER: What are you going to do – eat it, or talk to it?

EGON: What's the best way to keep flies out of the kitchen?

RAY: Put a corpse in the lounge.

PETER: Did you hear about Gormless Gussie?

WINSTON: No. What about her?

PETER: She slept with her head under the pillow.

WINSTON: What happened?

PETER: The fairies took all her teeth out!

PETER: Say you'll marry me, Florence.

FLORENCE: Get lost, Pete.

PETER: Oh, go on, Florence. I'm crazy about you . . . I worship the ground you creep on . . . Why, if you don't marry me, I'll hang myself from that big oak tree on your front lawn!

FLORENCE: Don't be a drag, Pete. You know my father told you not to hang around our place . . .

EGON: I need something for my kidney, Doc.

DOCTOR: Okay – here's a pound of steak, go make yourself a pie!

74

RAY: I think psychiatry is a load of junk.

WINSTON: What makes you say that, Ray?

RAY: Well, I went to my psychiatrist today, and he told me I was in love with my umbrella.

WINSTON: That does sound rather far-fetched.

RAY: I mean, I am very fond of my umbrella, and we have repect for each other, and I take it out on dates now and then. But *love* . . . that's just ridiculous!

Janine was walking along the beach the other day, stopping every now and then to kneel down and peer closely at the sand.

'Can I help you?' a lifeguard asked her. 'I presume you've lost something.'

'That's right,' said Janine. 'It's my boyfriend, Elton. I buried him in the sand, and now I can't find him.'

'But surely you can remember where you were sitting?' said the lifeguard.

'Don't be an idiot,' snapped Janine. 'Can *you* remember where you were sitting this time last year?'

POLICEMAN: I'm afraid you've been acting very suspiciously, and I'm going to lock you up for the night.

PETER: What's the charge?

POLICEMAN: Oh, no charge, sir – it's all part of the service.

PSYCHIATRIST: What seems to be the trouble?

PETER: I keep having this urge to cover myself all over with gold paint.

PSYCHIATRIST: I see . . . Well, I think we can safely say that you are suffering from a gilt complex.

JANINE: Like a rock-cake?

RAY: Thanks – mind if I take my pick?

RAY: Hey, Janine, which two letters of the alphabet are corroded?

JANINE: I don't know.

RAY: D K.

Winston went into a butcher's shop, and was horrified to see human heads, arms, torsos and legs of all sizes hanging on hooks.

'Why, this is terrible!' cried Winston. 'What are you, a mass-murderer?'

The butcher scowled at him. 'What's the matter – have you never been in a family butcher's shop before?'

PETER: Who's that down in the cellar, clanking chains?

GHOSTS: We're just a gang of ghosts, sir, and we mean no harm to man nor beast.

PETER: Oh. How did you die, by the way?

GHOSTS: 'Tis a tragic tale, sir. We were all sailors, you see. One day the captain of our ship died, and we had to bury him . . .

PETER: Yes, go on . . .

GHOSTS: Well, our captain had told us if he died then we were to bury him at sea. And sure, the twenty eight of us perished trying to dig his grave . . .

Egon was strolling along a country lane, on one of his fungus-collecting trips, when he saw an old lady holding two kettles up to her ears. Every few minutes she gave a little cheer and a jump of excitement.

'Excuse me,' said Egon. 'Would you mind telling me what you're doing?'

'Well,' said the old lady. 'If you hold two kettles up to your ears, you can hear the sound of a football match.'

Intrigued, Egon took the two kettles and held them up to his ears. He stood like this for a few minutes, feeling somewhat foolish and hearing nothing from the kettles.

'*I* can't hear anything,' said Egon.

'Ha-hah!' cackled the old lady. 'It must be half-time . . .'

WINSTON: What's that iron box over there for?

PETER: That's my new pillow.

WINSTON: Pillow? Won't it be rather hard?

PETER: What do you think I am, Winston – an idiot? I'm going to stuff it with feathers before I use it.

RAY: Why didn't they bury the Duke of Wellington with full military honours in 1847?

EGON: Because he didn't die until 1852.

EGON: What will the first clock on the moon be called?

RAY: A lunar-tic.

81

Winston was on a case in Egypt, involving a ghost of Pharaoh's tomb who was homesick for his mummy. While he was there, Winston decided to visit the local bazaar to see if he could pick up some bargains in antiques.

'How about this, sir,' said one stall-owner. 'The authentic skull of Moses.'

'Too expensive for me,' said Winston.

'Then how about this skull,' said the owner, producing another one. 'This is much cheaper, because it's smaller – the authentic skull of baby Moses!'

RAY: I've just been to see my financial advisor.

EGON: Really? How are things?

RAY: Pretty good. It seems that I've got enough money to last me the rest of my life. Providing . . .

EGON: Yes – providing what?

RAY: Providing I die by four o'clock this afternoon!

WINSTON: I've just been to get some fish and chips, but gave up after queing for half an hour. Why is that shop always so crowded?

RAY: I guess the fish fillet.

When Winston first came to London, he hopped on a bus and asked the conductor:

'Will this bus take me to Oxford Street?'

'Which part?' said the conductor.

'Why – all of me!' said Winston.

RAY: Why was the hatstand in the hall?

PETER: Because it had nowhere to sit.

PETER: Just now I saw fifteen planks standing in a circle.

WINSTON: How extraordinary!

PETER: Not really; they were just having a board meeting.

WINSTON: Have a good holiday, Janine?

JANINE: No, it was rotten. Pelted with rain every day.

WINSTON: Well, you certainly managed to get a fabulous sun-tan.

JANINE: That's not a sun-tan, Winston . . . that's *rust!*

PSYCHIATRIST: You'll be glad to know, Slimer, that you haven't got an inferiority complex after all.

SLIMER: Gluggle . . . no, doc?

PSYCHIATRIST: No. The fact is, you *are* inferior!

PETER:	I suppose you've saved quite a few people's lives down here at the beach this summer?
LIFEGUARD:	Oh, yes – dozens.
PETER:	And have you saved any girls?
LIFEGUARD:	Yes, about twenty.
PETER:	Really? Do you think I could have one?

RAY:	What dance do the cleaners of this building do?
JANINE:	I don't know. Surprise me.
RAY:	The char-char.

ESKIMO:	I just don't understand it. I installed radiators in my kayak and immediately it went up in flames! How do you explain that?
PETER:	Simple, friend. You can't have your kayak and heat it!

PETER: You know Delores, I used to be an eight-stone weakling.

DELORES: Really, Pete?

PETER: Yep. Whenever I went to the beach with my girlfriend, this fourteen-stone bully used to come over and kick sand in my face. So I took the famous Claude Atlas body-building course. In just a short while I weighed fourteen stone and bulged with muscles.

DELORES: Then what happened?

PETER: The next time I went to the beach with my girlfriend a *twenty-one* stone bully came over and kicked sand in my face!

RAY: Can I join you in a cup of coffee?

JANINE: Push off! There's not enough room.

EGON: I've got a headache. Will you give me some prepared acetylsalicylic acid, please?

CHEMIST: Do you mean aspirin, sir?

EGON: Yes, that's the stuff. I can never remember its name!

JANINE: You're really stupid, Ray.

RAY: What makes you say that?

JANINE: I've just heard that you went to that new mind-reader for a consultation – and she only charged you half-price!

EGON: What's a vampire's favourite dance?
PETER: The fang-dango.

Slimer struck up a friendship with another ghoul, who was almost as thick as himself. They went into a pub, and started to have a game of snooker. After an hour neither had scored a single point. The ghoul whispered to Slimer:

'We're never going to finish this game if we carry on like this. Let's cheat.'

'Bloob?' mumbled Slimer, with a puzzled frown. 'How?'

'Let's take away the wooden triangle . . .'

JANINE: Excuse me, do you think you could take that dress out of the window, please?

SHOP GIRL: Which one, madam?

JANINE: The orange thing, with the turquoise stripes and purple polka dots.

SHOP GIRL: Certainly, madam. I'll take it out now.

JANINE: Thanks a lot. The wretched thing annoys me every time I pass your shop!

EGON: It's such a nice day. I think I'll take Slimer to the zoo.

JANINE: Why bother? If they want the creepy little monster, let them come and collect him.

1ST VAMPIRE:	I'm bored.
2ND VAMPIRE:	Me too. Let's play a game. How about 'Mountain Massacres'?
1ST VAMPIRE:	How do you play that?
2ND VAMPIRE:	Oh, for pretty high stakes.

MUSICIAN:	Excuse me, can you tell me how I can get to the Royal Festival Hall?
PETER:	Practise, man, practise!

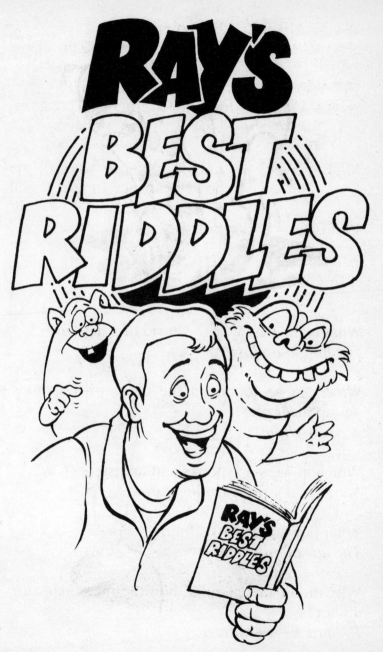

RAY'S BEST RIDDLES

What is the best way to get rid of a demon?
Tell him to do his exorcises.

What can be found on the cover of a spook's pin-up magazine?
A cover-ghoul.

Which flowers do spooks and monsters grow?
Mari-ghouls and morning gories.

What law do all ghosts follow?
The law of grave-ity.

Why didn't the cannibal boil the missionary for dinner?
Because he was a fryer.

What injury do Olympic athletes suffer?
Slipped discus.

If the Marquis de Sade were alive today, what would he be famous for?
Old age.

Why did the very fat ghost go on a diet?
She wanted to keep her ghoulish figure.

What is the favourite sport of an executioner?
Sleighing.

What do sea-monsters like to eat?
Fish and ships.

What has become the most expensive vehicle to operate?
A supermarket shopping-trolley.

How does a monster count to 25?
On its fingers.

What is a monster's usual eyesight?
20-20-20-20-20-20-20.

What are a dog's clothes made of?
Some mutt-erial or other.

Why did the animal lover call his dog 'Aversion'?
Everybody has a pet aversion.

What would you get if you crossed the Frankenstein monster with a hot dog?
A Frankfurterstein.

What happens to you if you get hit by a Wells Fargo express wagon?
You'd be stage-struck.

What happened when the prisoners in Dartmoor put on a play?
It was a cell-out.

What did the first herring say to the second herring?
'Am I my brother's kipper?'

What was the vampire doing on the dual-carriageway?
Looking for the main arterial road.

What's the best way to cut down on pollution in schools?
Use unleaded pencils.

What happens when you slip on thin ice?
Your bottom gets thaw.

What was Dr Jeckyll's favourite game?
Hyde and Shriek.

Where does a ghost keep its car?
In a mirage.

Who are the slowest talkers in the world?
Convicts – they can spent 25 years on a single sentence.

What do you call a ten-ton monster with seven heads?
'Your majesty . . . .'

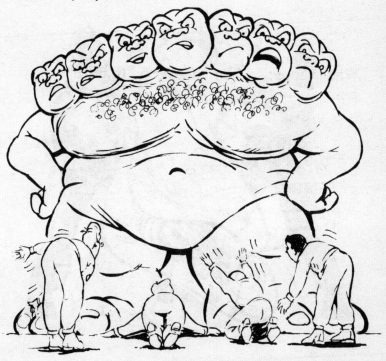

What did the peel say to the banana?
'Don't move – I've got you covered!'

Why doesn't it pay to talk to anyone who has four lips?
All you'll get is a load of double-talk.

Why did James Bond spray his room with DDT?
He thought there was a bug hidden in it.

What happened when the police caught the hamburger?
They took it to the station and grilled it.

Who is the thirstiest person in the world?
The one who drank Canada Dry.

What song does a violinist sing to his instrument?
'I've Got You Under My Chin . . .'

Why did the teacher let the glow worm go to the toilet?
Because when you gotta glow, you've gotta glow.

What happened to the man who took a dive from 200 ft. into a glass of orange juice?
Nothing; it was a soft drink.

What did the comedian say when he took off all his clothes?
'What's the matter – have you never seen a comic strip before?

What do you get if you cross a canary with an elephant?
An extremely messy cage.

Why was the light bulb interested in the light switch?
Because it turned him on.

How do you find a barber who's gone missing?
Comb the city.

Why can't you trust fishermen and shepherds?
They live by hook and by crook.

Where do geologists go for entertainment?
Rock concerts.

If a rodent crosses the road, rolls in some mud
and crosses back again, what do you call it?
A dirty double-crossing rat.

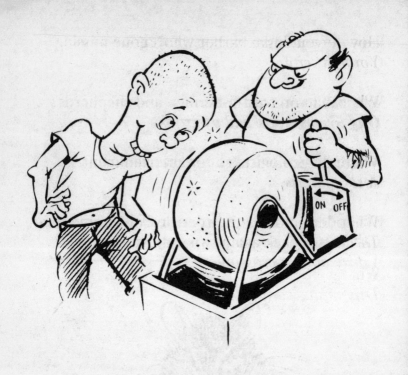

Why did the stupid spook put his head against the grindstone?
To sharpen his wits.

Why did the stupid spook refuse to use toothpaste?
He insisted that his teeth weren't loose.

What caused a mass riot in the post office?
A stamp-ede.

How do you kiss a hockey player?
You pucker up.

What is an organic farmer?
One who tills it like it is.

Who talks for workers in a bicycle factory?
A spokesman.

What's the most popular gardening magazine?
The Weeder's Digest.

What's the best way to see flying saucers?
Trip up the waitress.

Where do hikers keep their sleeping pills?
In their nap-sacks.

How do you make a poisonous snake cry?
Take away his rattle.

What's the best thing for persistent nail-biting?
Sharp teeth.

How many different kind of guns are there?
Two; good guns and bad guns.

—THE LAST REVOLTING DOLLOP— OF SLIMER'S GHOULISH GAGS

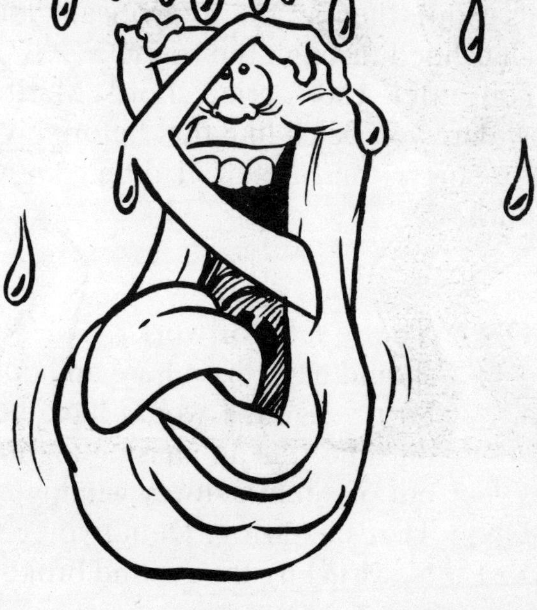

At a very refined cocktail party, Lord Marlborough was horrified when Peter took a deep swig of his drink, then let out a terrifically loud belch which echoed through the room.

'You utter cad!' cried Lord Marlborough. 'How dare you belch like that before my wife!'

'I'm sorry,' said Peter. 'I didn't know it was her turn.'

EGON: You're late for work again, Ray. You should have been here an hour ago.

RAY: Sorry, Egon. I would have been here on time, but in chasing a ghost, I fell out of a tenth-storey window.

EGON: That's amazing. Didn't you get hurt?

RAY: No. Luckily the ground broke my fall.

PETER: I've just been ghost-busting in Africa.

WINSTON: Congratulations. How did it go?

PETER: Okay. You know, I met this weird tribe of cannibals in the Omboko district. They've come up with this brand-new food idea. They take a human hand, chop it into pieces, and let it dry in the sun for ages. Then they grind the pieces into powder, put it into bottles and sell it. All you have to do is add milk to the powder.

WINSTON: Sounds awful. What do they call it?

PETER: A hand-shake.

EGON: Quick, Janine – call me a taxi!

JANINE: You're a taxi.

PETER: Did you hear what happened when Slimer went to Hampton Court Maze?

JANINE: No, what happened?

PETER: He got lost for six hours trying to find the way *in*.

WINSTON: How can you tell the time without looking at your watch?

RAY: Easy. Just eat an apple and count the pips.

EGON: Which candles burn longer – wax or tallow?

PETER: Neither; both burn shorter.

BABY
VAMPIRE: Mummy, mummy – what's a vampire?

MOTHER
VAMPIRE: Shut up and eat your soup before it clots.

WINSTON: I'll have you know I come from a very old family. One of my ancestors died at Waterloo.

RAY: Really – which platform?

SLIMER: Umm . . . glog . . . I'm nobody's fool!

JANINE: Well, Slimer, maybe someone will adopt you.

WINSTON: Hey, Egon – what happened to that unbreakable, shockproof, waterproof, anti-magnetic, rustproof, laser-operated, everlasting watch you had?

EGON: I lost it.

PETER: Egon, where do you take your baths?

EGON: In the spring.

PETER: I said 'where', not '*when*'.

RAY: Can you lend me 10 pence? I want to phone a friend.

PETER: Here's 20 pence. Phone them all.

RAY: I see you've got musical feet, Janine.

JANINE: What are you talking about?

RAY: Well, they're both flat.

GIRL: My Daddy takes things apart to see why they won't go.
RAY: So what?
GIRL: So you'd better go!

JANINE: I had a pet parrot for over a year and it never said a single word.
EGON: How odd. Perhaps it was tongue-tied.
JANINE: No, I don't think so.
EGON: Or maybe it was just shy.
JANINE: No, I don't think so.
EGON: Then why *didn't* the parrot say anything?
JANINE: It was stuffed.

Ray was taken by a friend to a secret seance. When they arrived, the shifty-looking medium asked Ray if there was anybody special he would like to contact and speak to.

'Yes,' said Ray. 'I'd like to speak to my grandfather Moses.'

'It can be arranged,' said the medium. Then he went into a deep trance; he started moaning and groaning, and his voice started to change into an ancient croak, 'Ray . . . this is your grandfather Moses, speaking from Heaven . . . It's marvellous up here . . . Is there anything you'd like to ask me, my child?'

'Yes, there is, Grandfather,' smiled Ray. 'How come you're in Heaven when you're not even dead yet?'

PETER: My mother lives on a houseboat
            now.
WINSTON: What's it like?
PETER: Super. If she ever runs short of
            money, it's so easy to pop over to
            the bank!